D0596680

GENDER

A CONVERSATION GUIDE
FOR PARENTS AND PASTORS

BRIAN SEAGRAVES
& HUNTER LEAVINE

Gender: A Conversation Guide for Parents and Pastors
© Brian Seagraves and Hunter Leavine/TGBC 2018

Published by: The Good Book Company
Tel (US): 866 244 2165
Tel (UK): 0333 123 0880
Email (US): info@thegoodbook.com
Email (UK): info@thegoodbook.co.uk

Websites:
North America: www.thegoodbook.com
UK: www.thegoodbook.co.uk
Australia: www.thegoodbook.com.au
New Zealand: www.thegoodbook.co.nz

Previously published as *Gender: Conversation Guide
(Building Foundations)* by Acacia Books

ISBN: 9781784983505 | Printed in Denmark

Cover design by Dane Low/The Good Book Company

CONTENTS

INTRODUCTION

The world around us is changing quickly, and it is difficult to find clarity about some of life's most important issues. Whether you are a parent, mentor, pastor, youth minister, children's-ministry volunteer, or simply a friend, we wrote this book to help you bring clarity to young minds in a world that is spinning in confusion.

Although our world is filled with many challenges, this is the world in which God has placed us. Psalm 139 tells us that we are each knit together in our mother's womb. We are creations of God himself. In Job 14 v 5 we are told that our days are determined by God and not by chance. When these two important truths are placed together, we can see that God has not only chosen to create us, but he has also chosen *when* we would be created. It is important that we understand we are living in this time for a specific purpose. Jesus calls his followers to be a light where God has placed us, and to glorify him with how we live our lives in this world.

The confusion we experience in this life is not from the absence of God, but because of the consequences of sin. In the same way that pain is a signal alerting us that something in our bodies isn't right, the pain and suffering in our world is a signal that something is broken. As Christian people, we need to speak with great clarity, compassion, and conviction about where the brokenness in our world comes from—sin.

In John 17 Jesus prays that his disciples would not be taken out of the world, but that they would be protected from "the evil one" (v 15) If Jesus' prayer is that his disciples stand strong in his truth, then our prayer for our children, family, friends, and even ourselves should be the same.

We are not called to *hide* from the world, or to blend in with the world; we are called to stand out. In order to grow to become distinctive disciples, we need to be able to have meaningful and deep conversations that explore difficult subjects and questions in the light of God's word.

In particular, there is a collective responsibility within the church to bring children up with clarity about who God is and what he has said. Furthermore, we have to raise our children in the world the way it is, not the way we would like it to be.

Consider God's word to Moses in Deuteronomy:

> *You shall therefore lay up these words of mine in your heart and in your soul, and you shall bind*

them as a sign on your hand, and they shall be as
frontlets between your eyes. You shall teach them to
your children, talking of them when you are sitting
in your house, and when you are walking by the way,
and when you lie down, and when you rise. You shall
write them on the doorposts of your house and on your
gates, that your days and the days of your children may
be multiplied in the land that the Lord swore to your
fathers to give them, as long as the heavens are above
the earth.   *Deuteronomy 11 v 18-21*

We are called not only to hold tightly to God's word, but to pass it along to the ones we love. It is not only something we should cherish, but also something which should be carried to the next generation.

The goal of this book is to help build strong foundations in children and young people that are rooted in God's truth and connected to the gospel. As the world is changing, we do not need to flee, but rather point to Jesus himself, who is both the truth and the life (John 14 v 6).

In a world cluttered with opinions about gender, sexuality, race, and truth, we don't need to be louder; we need to be clearer. We need to be compelling and competent to answer the questions that face the next generation, and to do so in a way that is loving intelligent and honoring to God.

Our prayer is that this resource would not only help in the discipling of your loved ones, but that it would also help in your own understanding of God's word. Let's be a people who take God's word seriously enough to teach it at every age, and let's teach it with great intentionality.

Brian Seagraves and Hunter Leavine
April 2018

GENDER: THE WHY

Before we dive in, it is important to first start with the "why."

"Why should we care about gender at all?"
"Is what we believe about gender really that important?"
"Is this an issue that should matter to everyone?"

Without understanding the "why," we will be tempted to slip into silence on the topic, or even worse, slip away from what God's word says. If we do not take building foundations seriously, our children can fall into two massive dangers.

TWO MASSIVE DANGERS

1. The Danger of Misplaced Identity

Have you noticed that our culture discusses hot-button issues differently than it did ten years ago? It seems that people are much quicker to label disagreement as "hatred" or "bigotry." Failing to affirm what someone believes or does can often be taken as failing to love them at all.

While there are many reasons for this, the main reason is that society has bought into the lie that people are what they believe and what they do.

Think about it: if this is true and someone critiques your beliefs, you're much more likely to consider a mere rejection of ideas as a rejection of you personally.

For example, someone who is gay can easily interpret the condemnation of homosexual activity as a rejection of themselves. This happens when our identity is based on anything—our desires, attractions, skin color, or actions—other than what God's word says.

It's not just children who want to fit in with their peers; we all do. We all have a longing to be loved and accepted. Often, our fallenness leads us to want to be accepted *for* our brokenness, not in spite of it. Our identity can become based on things directly opposed to God's design.

The antidote to this problem is the gospel, where we find acceptance by God in the midst of our brokenness, not because of it; we find fulfillment that was elusive when we tried to locate our identity and self-worth internally.

When our identity is based on anything other than being an adopted and ransomed child of God, we stand awaiting an inevitable fall. We need to understand what it means to have been intentionally designed and saved by God, or we may let our striving to find our self-worth elsewhere push us away from our Creator.

The gospel—the good news about Jesus' work on the cross—not only gives us a new identity but also a new community. Within the community of the church, we can find clarity about some of life's most important issues, as well as support, as we seek to honor God in a world that is plagued by sin and confusion. No matter what is happening in the world, we can find comfort knowing that as people who have been purchased by the work of Christ, we always have a home in his church.

2. The Danger of Unrecognized Authority

God's word should be the lens through which we view the world around us, and it should be the ultimate authority of our lives. Our beliefs, thoughts, and actions should be shaped by what the Bible teaches.

Every day we are tempted to allow the world to shape the way we see God's word, rather than allow God's word to shape the way we see the world. It is crucial that the ever-changing views of the world are not allowed to affect the way we understand the everlasting truth of God's word. There is too much at stake.

The danger is not just that we might "get gender wrong," or that someone we love might become gender-confused, but rather, that a wedge might be placed between our lives and God's word. If we choose not to believe what God's word says about gender, we should not be too surprised when we choose not to believe God's word at all.

When we start to pick and choose when to accept the authority of God's word, we are standing on a slippery slope; if one part is rejected, we will struggle to hold on to any of it. How we think and talk about gender is connected to our view of God's word as a whole.

We all live in a world that is vying not only for our *attention* but also our *allegiance*. This sets Christians—especially children—up for an inevitable collision. When two objects collide, the stronger prevails over the weaker.

In a very real way, our children need to be trained to handle the strongest assault the world will bring, and yet remain committed to God's word. You and your children need this book because, while statistically it is unlikely that your children will become transgender themselves, it is assured that they will have to decide who they stand with on the questions of gender and authority. There are only two options: stand with God or stand against him.

HOW TO USE THIS GUIDE

WHO IS THIS GUIDE FOR?

We have created this guide for anyone who works with children and teens. Whether you are a church worker, relative, parent or friend, we believe that this will be a helpful tool for you on a very important topic. Although anyone can benefit from this guide, we address parents throughout the guide for simplicity's sake. It is up to you to take this and translate it into your context, and we hope that it will help you begin to speak clearly in our world today.

THE ROLE OF THE CHURCH AND PARENTS

There is a collective responsibility within the community of believers to bring children up with clarity. One of the blessings of being part of the church is that we do not have to go through life alone. We do not have to fear asking for help, and we can learn from and work with one another to build foundations centered on the gospel and directed by God's word. When the church partners with families, children and students are most likely to flourish. Involvement in a local church is one of the most important factors in building strong foundations, and it is a blessing we all should seek.

PART ONE: FOUNDATIONS

In Part One the content has been divided into three main "foundations." The foundations roughly align with pre-school (up to 7 years old), elementary (7-11 years old), and middle/high school (12-18 years).

You will benefit from reading all three foundations, regardless of your child's age. For example, if your child is elementary aged you will want to use the age tips and discussion questions found in the second foundation. However, you will be helped by knowing what is coming in the next foundation before your child gets there.

Key Concepts and Passages

Key concepts are found in each foundation, and guidance on areas of conversation. Important Bible passages to discuss are found on page 51. Common ideas and themes build cumulatively from one foundation to the next and are most helpful when taught together. Within "Key Concepts", there will be some terminology that might be helpful when communicating to that particular age group.

Sample dialogue with the child will be in this paragraph style.

Age Tips

There are both unique opportunities and challenges at each age. The age-tips section lists some specific suggestions for addressing children at each level of development, and includes some important Bible passages that you will want to read and talk about with them.

Questions and Discussion Starters

Each foundation will also include age-specific questions and discussion starters that can be launchpads for more conversation. The goal is not to have a single conversation, but rather, to have ongoing discussions with your children and teens. This section will help you keep the conversation alive.

PART TWO: TOOLBOX

Part Two is a toolbox of helpful resources that contains a variety of short sections to better equip you as an adult to navigate this issue in today's society.

This Guide is Intended to be a Tool, Not a Crutch

Our desire is that this guide would serve as a tool to help you have conversations relevant to our world today that are deeply rooted in God's word. We do not, however, want this to be a crutch. This guide should supplement the work you are already doing in discipling your child—reading Bible stories with them, praying with and for them, enjoying church life together, and finding opportunities to serve together.

Building foundations can be hard work. It does not happen overnight, and it requires a big-picture perspective that looks to the future. While God's word never changes, our contexts will look different. We want to encourage you to actively think about how you can bring biblical clarity to your children in whatever situation you find yourself.

FOUNDATION ONE

PRESCHOOL AND YOUNG CHILDREN (UP TO 7 YEARS)

KEY CONCEPTS

God Is the Good Creator: Genesis 1 – 3

A clear understanding of gender is connected to having a good understanding of creation. It is important that parents help children understand that everything in the entire universe was created by God.

> *God made everything. This means that God made everything from the tiniest bug to the largest star. Everything he made in his creation should make us think about him.*

As children grow older and learn about the intricacies of God's creation, we should use those moments to point to the grandness and wonder of God's design. Talking about God as the designer of bugs, flowers, and forests, as well as the vastness of space, will help form a view of an intentional God who is active in the details of life.

Constantly talking about God as the Creator will help children begin to build trust in how God created every individual, including themselves.

Children also need to know that God is the *good* Creator.

> *The Bible tells us in Genesis 1 that, in the very beginning, God looked at his creation and said it was "good." God was happy with his creation, and he did not make any mistakes. Every star, tree, and animal was made exactly like God wanted it. Our hair color, skin color, freckles, and whether we are a boy or a girl are all a part of the wonderful way God made us to be.*

As children begin to first explore God's creation, they need to understand that it is *good*. It will not only help them have awe, respect, and love for God's design, but it will increase their trust in the way God designed it. Understanding God's design will pave the way for understanding sin—what happens when we go outside of God's good design..

God Is Your Personal Creator

Sometimes it is easier for people to believe that God created what they see in the night sky than what they see when they look in the mirror. Viewing God as a *personal* Creator is crucial.

Not only did God look at his creation and say it was "good," but when God looked at the first people, he said they were "very good." People are the most important part of God's creation. He cares about every single person deeply.

Because God is your Creator, and because God cares about you, God knows your name. God knows what you look like. He knows that you are a boy/girl; he even knows the things you like. God knows everything about you because he made you!

As children first begin to learn about God, it is important that they have this foundation of seeing God not just as a "good Creator," but also *their* personal Creator—a God who knows them and loves them. The fact that the same God who made the universe is the same God who "knitted me together in my mother's womb" should never cease to amaze us (Psalm 139 v 13).

If we are not intentional about reinforcing this message, we can easily begin to see God as a distant, impersonal Creator. However, that is not the type of Creator who "walked" in the garden with Adam and Eve, cared about the murder of Abel, and worked to help Noah build the ark. The God of the Bible is not an impersonal God. As we walk our children through God's word, we must be intentional in highlighting God's personal involvement in the lives of his people.

This will connect with future sections that show that

God cares about our personal lives, personally determined our gender, and doesn't make any mistakes.

God Gave Us His Word: 2 Timothy 3 v 16

At the center of the conversation around gender are these questions: "What do we make of God's word?" "Is Scripture really from God?" "What kind of authority does the Bible have over my life?" "Can I trust the Bible even when it does not align with what the world says?" In order to build a truly strong foundation in the lives of our children, we have to tackle this matter head on.

We can know about God because he has told us about himself in the Bible. God gave us the Bible as a gift because he wants us to understand more about him, about ourselves, and about what he wants. God is always busy looking after everything he has made, and he cares about his people.

The Bible is not a rule book or a book filled only with "good ideas." The Bible is God speaking to us.

From a young age, for better or for worse, children begin to form their ideas about the Bible. As we work with young children, we need to think about this process and how it comes into play later in life.

If we treat the Bible just like a rule book, they will be shaped to see it as cold and impersonal. If we just treat the Bible like an adventure novel, they will be shaped to see it as an accumulation of entertaining and inspirational stories. If we don't talk with our children about the Bible at all, then they will be shaped to see it as irrelevant. We need to understand that how we handle Scripture with our children when they are young will shape how they see Scripture in the future.

As we teach young children God's word, we need to help them understand that when they go to God's word, they can understand more about him and his creation, including themselves.

We get to know God through the Bible!

The Bible is a big true story. It tells us what God has done in the world from the time he made everything until now. It tells us about good things that will help us, and bad things that will hurt us. It tells us how we can say "thank you" to God for all the wonderful things he has done. We thank him by doing what he says. God's word is not just something you learn when you're young. You learn from it and love it when you are grown up too.

Encouraging your child to both understand and trust God's word will help them navigate their way through the world's doubt about the Bible, and the world's claims to have a "better truth." It's been said that if you want to teach a bank teller how to spot a counterfeit, you don't show them every counterfeit there is, but rather you have them handle the real thing. If they know intimately what *real* money looks like, then they will know a counterfeit when they see it. That approach is needed for young children. If we help them start "handling" God's truth while they are young, it will help them spot lies as they encounter them in the future.

This begins with regular Bible-reading and scripture memorization; it should also include setting an example for them to see what it looks like to love and trust God's word. There is too much at stake not to take Scripture seriously.

Sin Is Not Following God's Word

It is never too early to help children begin to understand sin. Although many choose to avoid talking about sin with young children, it is important that they begin to understand that God's good design has been impacted by sin.

Even though God made people exactly how he wanted, we all still choose not to do what he asks us to do. When we don't listen to God and we don't do what he says, that is called "sin". When we don't want what God wants, that is sin too. Because of our sin, we can't be God's friends. People are separated from him.

When we discuss sin with children, it needs to be in an age-appropriate way. They do not need to understand all the intricacies of it, but it is important to begin the conversation when they are young.

Discussing sin with young children will help them see

that although God is the designer of creation, not all is as it should be. Creation is beautiful in many ways, but sin has caused creation to "groan" (Romans 8 v 22). As children get older, they will see these broken pieces of God's creation and begin to ask, "Why is it this way?" The answer is not the absence of God, but rather the presence of sin.

> *When we sin, we hurt other people, and we hurt ourselves. When we go outside of God's design, we get hurt. When something is not right, it is not because God is not there; it is because sin is there.*
>
> *God sees the hurt people in the world and has done something about it. He sent Jesus to fix it. And one day God will make everything all right again. It can be hard to live in a broken world, but we need to trust in him, even when things feel bad.*

Understanding sin will also help children begin to see that regardless of what sin they are entangled in, each and every one of us is in need of God's grace.

> *It is not good that things are broken, and not right that people get hurt. Only God can fix what is broken. We all need God's help.*
>
> *What is something that you can't do alone? Maybe it is something that is too heavy to lift, or too high to reach. Just as there are simple things that we cannot do alone, there are big, important things that we cannot do alone. The biggest most important thing we need is something*

> *we cannot do. It's this: to make a way to become God's friend. We can't do that because of our sin.*
>
> *But Jesus can do that. The wonderful thing about the Bible is that all of it tells us about who Jesus is and what he has done for us, so that we can be friends with God forever. The Bible helps us learn about Jesus so we can trust him and be thankful for him.*

Understanding our need for God's grace will help us later show and give grace to others. That simple principle can and should be taught when children are young.

JESUS

At the heart of the Bible is the Savior Jesus.

> *No matter how much sin hurts people, and breaks and spoils our world, Jesus is greater and stronger. He will make everything right again.*

Jesus was an important part of the creation process. Colossians 1 v 16 tells us:

> *For by him [Jesus] all things were created, in heaven and on earth, visible and invisible, whether thrones or dominions or rulers or authorities—all things were created through him and for him.*

> *Jesus was together with God in the beginning when God made everything. They made it all together. And Jesus is still with God looking after creation today. Jesus was with God when you and I were made. Like God, Jesus cares deeply about all his creation.*

Our children can be taught that Jesus created and cares for his creation, so much so that he would give his life to see it saved from sin. Children might not be able to grasp all of this at first, but that should not discourage us from pointing them to the gospel.

AGE TIPS

- *Your child may not understand* what it means for God to be totally good or for him to have created the universe, and that's perfectly okay. If they learn these foundational concepts when they are young, they will grow to understand them in all their fullness as they get older.
- *Talk with your child regularly about how God knows them and loves them.* Tell them that God knows what they look like because he created them. Tell them that God made their hair the way it is, and he made them look the way they do. This will help reinforce that their sex/gender is not a mistake, but rather a gift created by God.
- *Don't be afraid to introduce the concept of sin to young children.* They need to understand that we can know what God says, but we often do the wrong thing.

- *Begin to teach your children about our responsibility for our sin and the results of living in a sinful world.* While it is important to help them begin to have a framework for understanding that we are surrounded by sin and brokenness, sin is not something that only exists outside of us. We are *all* sinful and are responsible for our rebellious hearts towards God. At the same time, we experience the results of the sins of others and the general brokenness of the natural world. We are not the way we should be, and the world is not the way it should be. We are responsible when we choose to disobey what God has commanded, and we experience pain and confusion because the world is not the way it should be as a result of sin.

- *Show how God's word and the Bible story is exciting.* Children don't just wake up one day and think that the Bible is "boring" or "outdated." They are shaped to see God's word that way. However, children need to be helped to see that the Bible is an exciting story about God working in the world through Jesus. The Bible is a special gift from God himself, and the Bible is an opportunity to know about the most important thing in the whole universe—God. We get to be explorers of God's word. We should be more excited to learn about the Creator of the universe than anything else in it.

- *God is good even when we feel bad.* It can be hard to trust that God is good when we or our children suffer from sickness or disability. When we strive to walk by faith and not by sight, we understand from scripture that while God made creation good, it has begun to decay. Sin and the fall touches every area of life in this world. Every sickness, hurt, and disability is a painful reminder of this. But far from leading us to despair, it should lead us to long for the day when Jesus comes back to gather his people, heal every hurt, and wipe every tear from our eyes.

QUESTIONS AND DISCUSSION STARTERS

- Tell your child that mommy is a girl, and daddy is a boy.
- Explain the two genders, and ask your child what gender people are.
- When your child discovers something new in the world (like flowers, the moon, an animal) tell them God made it, and ask what other things God made.
- Have conversations about different things that God created. When your child is playing with an animal, a toy, or something that they picked up outside, talk with them about how God created that, or created the people who made it. If God created every single little bug, then we can believe that he created you and me, and that he paid attention to even the tiniest details.

- Have conversations about how good God is. It is important for children to understand that God loves his creation and called his creation "good."

FOUNDATION TWO

ELEMENTARY AGE
(7-11 YEARS)

KEY CONCEPTS

God Loves Males and Females Equally, But they are Intentionally Different

Foundation One covered God being the good creator. Every inch of creation was made by God with purpose. As your child begins to interact more with other children, it is important that they understand that God created males and females to be equal but different. We see this from the very first moments of creation.

An important part of the creation account is the distinct lines God draws between males and females. When talking to children about how God created Adam and Eve, do not shy away from the differences we see in the text.

Genesis 1 v 27 tells us that…

God created man in his own image,
in the image of God he created him;
male and female he created them.

Gender is actually part of the original creation design; this should not be overlooked. Because God gave us the Bible, we can trust that everything in the Bible is there for a reason.

In the story of the creation of Adam and Eve in Genesis chapter 2, Adam was formed from dust from the ground. This is similar imagery to that of a potter creating a vase. Then, God breathed life into that dirt-vessel to create man. Once again, God is active in the details.

It is important to note that the story of Eve is different. God caused Adam to fall asleep; then he pulled a rib from Adam. From that rib he created Eve. Adam and Eve were both fully human. However, God created them differently.

There are two important points to be made from this somewhat strange story.

First, there was a distinctive difference in the creation of Adam (male) and the creation of Eve (female). If God had wanted to, he could have created both from the dust, but God chose to create them differently for a reason.

Second, God wanted Adam and Eve to be different, but to have a *relationship* with one another.

Adam and Eve's creation moment was special. God created humans to have a special kind of relationship with each other. There are differences between males and females, and God does not want them to be separate or to look down on each other.

> *God made boys and girls different, and it is okay that boys and girls are not the same. God created them to be different from one another on purpose. God's word is clear that there are right and wrong ways for boys and girls to treat each other.*
>
> *God loves boys and girls the same and wants them to treat each other with love, kindness, and respect.*

How we speak and interact with those of the opposite gender will say a lot to children who are watching. We need to look for ways to teach young boys and girls how to view and treat each other.

There are two principles here. First, we should respect, honour and value the differences there are between us. Men and boys should not ridicule girls for "girly" activities they do, and vice versa. Second, we should honour and promote diversity in expression of masculinity and femininity. After all Jacob stayed home and cooked (Genesis 25 v 29), and Jael put a tent peg through a man's head (Judges 4 v 21)!

Not Everyone Believes the Same Thing

Because we believe God is the good Creator, and because we believe God gave us his word, we believe what God's word says. Not everyone believes the same things, however.

By the time they are in elementary school, your child is starting to interact more and more with others from different backgrounds. It is important they understand that some people do not believe what you and your family believe.

While you don't want to scare or discourage your children, you need to be proactive in preparing them to handle disagreement in a gracious way. You want your children to hear about gender first from you, and you should also want to be the first to help them understand that others think differently. They need to know that you are not unaware of these issues.

One of the increasingly difficult realities about living as a Christian today is that many people find our beliefs to be hateful and intolerant. Sadly, this means you will be teaching your child ideas that, while true, could very well lead to them being criticized or called names. In Luke 14 v 25-33, Jesus tells the crowds to count the cost of following him, and we need to appreciate what fidelity to Christ may cost us and our children. Parents need to prepare their children not to find their identity in the approval of their classmates or friends. The fear

of man brings a snare (Proverbs 29 v 25), but the fear
of the Lord leads to wisdom (Proverbs 15 v 33).

> *Sometimes people will not believe the same thing as you and
> me, and that will make them upset. It is normal to want people
> to like you, but we need to first care about what God thinks.
> Even if certain people do not like what you believe, you can
> know you are loved by God and me.*
>
> *If we are always living to make people happy, we cannot
> follow Jesus well (Galatians 1 v 10).*

JESUS AND THE GOSPEL

Elementary school is a very important time for
children to begin to grasp not only their need but
also the world's true need for Jesus. During this time,
children begin to see the brokenness of the world
for themselves, and they also *begin* to understand the
concepts of sacrifice and sin. Whether in response to
hearing about a tragic event or a confusing discovery,
we need to draw a path for our children back to the
gospel—the good news of Jesus.

There can be a tendency for us to try to shelter
children from all of the brokenness of the world, and
while we certainly need to help them interact with
events and concepts at their level, we also need to be
willing to be real with them about some of life's most
challenging issues. Look for the opportunities, and do

not skirt the hard topics in life. Often times the hardest issues to talk about can be turned into the strongest bridges to Christ. If we leave some of life's most challenging questions unanswered and are unwilling to talk about some of the weighty things within the world, our children will grow up and look for answers elsewhere. Topics like natural disasters, school shootings, and world hunger cannot be fully understood apart from Scripture. The Bible does not ignore the results of a sin-torn world, and neither should we. These challenging issues should lead us to Scripture and ultimately to our hope in Christ.

As concerned as we might be about our children hearing the lies of the world, the center of our focus should always be pointing them to Jesus.

AGE TIPS

• *As best you can, model what it looks like for both genders to be equal but different.* Fathers, overtly love and respect your child's mother; don't ridicule your wife or girls because of their feminine characteristics. Biblical masculinity treasures and upholds women. Mothers, visibly respect your child's father and his leadership. Be supportive of your husband and boys being more physical in their play and hobbies than you may be. A lot of what children come to believe about gender and how the two genders should interact with each other will come from what they see in you.

- *Use movies and media as a springboard for discussion about gender and creation:* what was portrayed correctly? Incorrectly? Do not shy away from these unique conversations, but rather begin to be intentional and look for opportunities to have them with your children. This will help them learn to listen, think, and discuss important topics.

- As your child learns about dinosaurs, the earth, etc. in science class, *be involved in discussing either how those ideas fit or do not fit in a biblical worldview of creation.* Knowing what your children are learning in school is critical to your work in the home.

- *Encourage your child in their curiosity,* and help create an environment where investigating and asking questions is safe.

- *Ask when your child will be in a "health" class, and find out what will be taught.* You may want your child to be excused from that class, or you may just need to be prepared to discuss the topics before the class and when he/she comes home. Being proactive with gender and sexuality is always better than being reactive.

- As appropriate, *be open about areas of your life that you are working to align with God's design.*

- *Continue to build an awareness and understanding of the main points of Foundation One* in age-appropriate ways for your elementary-age child. They still need to hear that God is the good creator, that he knows us personally, and that sin is disobedience to God's word.

QUESTIONS AND DISCUSSION STARTERS

- Some people do not think God intentionally designed and created us or that he is at work today. Since they believe that, they likely believe our gender is the result of accident/chance. Do you know people who don't believe God created them? Why do they think that?

- What do you believe about the Bible?

- Since many people do not believe God has spoken in Scripture, they believe everyone decides for themselves how they should live. What do your friends believe about the Bible?

- How have you noticed that boys and girls behave differently? Or look different?

FOUNDATION THREE

MIDDLE OR HIGH-SCHOOL AGE (12+)

KEY CONCEPTS

We Trust God's Word over the Cultural Narrative

The question of authority is at the heart of any discussion about how people should act or see themselves. Everyone has an innate desire to fit in and be accepted, but before we adopt a position on an issue, we must first ask, "What does God's word say about this?"

All Scripture is God-breathed and is useful for teaching, rebuking, correcting, and training in righteousness (2 Timothy 3 v 16). Since Scripture is the very word of God, it should be our highest authority on all issues to which it speaks. Of course, non-Christians don't view the Bible this way, so it shouldn't surprise us when they believe differently.

The Bible does address gender, as has been seen in the previous foundations. And since it does, no amount of cultural pressure or disagreement should ever be enough to cause us to act or think contrary to God's word. This isn't to say that the Bible will always answer all of our questions; it won't. However, we can trust what it does state clearly, and rest in the fact that it's backed by the God of the universe.

Have you ever been in a situation where several people say conflicting things and you do not know who to trust? Maybe there was a dramatic incident at school and one friend was told what happened one way, and another said something completely different. When stories conflict, we are forced to answer the question, "Who do I trust?" Some people are tempted to just trust whatever is popular in the world; however, that often changes. Others are tempted to trust themselves, but our own understanding is often limited. As Christians, we can trust what God's word says because God is unchanging and all-knowing. God's word is often unpopular, but it is always right. This means that followers of Jesus don't just believe what everyone else believes. Instead we try to trust and obey God's word. Popular opinion is not the pursuit of a follower of Christ, faithfulness is. Jesus always loves us, and he is always with us. Knowing this will help us not to worry when other people don't like us because they don't agree with what we believe.

We Need to Trust God's Word over Our Feelings

It's not just culture and media that present contrary views to Scripture; our own thoughts and feelings often run contrary to the Bible as well. There is, perhaps, nothing we know as well or intimately as our own feelings; they are powerful. Sometimes they inform us correctly, but often times they do not. In a culture where "love" has been redefined to mean "agreement" or "support," Christians can struggle with feeling as though they aren't being loving if they disagree with someone else.

We must test everything—news stories, cultural talking-points, teachers, and even our feelings—against God's word. We often think our feelings must be trusted, but even these should be compared to Scripture, which says, "The heart is deceitful above all things, and desperately sick; who can understand it?" (Jeremiah 17 v 9).

Someone may feel that supporting a person or friend in their choice of gender identity is loving, but this feeling has misled them. It will never be loving to support something that God is against, and it will never be loving to encourage someone to act contrary to how God has designed them. As Christians, our first allegiance—indeed the greatest commandment—is to love God, and then, secondarily, people. True godly love for your neighbor will never entail encouraging them in behaviors that God condemns. Love often looks like telling people what they don't want to hear out of concern for their wellbeing.

But what if someone feels that they are a different gender than they are biologically? Every cell in each of our bodies has two chromosomes. With extremely rare exceptions, people are XX (female) or XY (male). So, even if someone feels confused about their gender, every cell in their body is of one, and only one, specific gender. Those cells are not confused.

The trend today is to say that when a person's self-image doesn't match their biology, it's the body that's wrong, not the psychology. We need to encourage people to align their gender identity and sense of self with what their physical self is. Encouraging the opposite will only lead to a greater sense of inner division.

There are individuals who struggle with something called "bodily integrity disorder." Some of these people feel that an arm or leg doesn't belong on their body. Should we encourage them to remove the arm/leg based on this feeling? No. A loving response will help the person see that the limb is a natural part of who they are, and they should work to align their feelings with their biology. The same holds true for those who struggle with an eating disorder. You don't tell the 95-pound (43kg) 16-year-old, "Your feelings are right; you are too fat." They need to see that their biology is not the problem, and we can help them work through their *feelings,* which are out of concert with their body.

Intersex People

Intersex people are individuals who have ambiguous genitalia or a mix of male and female genitalia, sex, internal sex organs, or chromosomes. Intersex people are frequently used as a "trump card" argument by pro-transgender people in this debate. Such people account for about 0.05 percent of the population, or 1 in 2,000 (according to isna.org).

As difficult as this situation is, the intersex comparison is a red herring—a distraction—to the transgender discussion. Why? Because transgender people do not have ambiguous genitals; they have clearly defined genitals, but they want to live in a way that doesn't match their physical makeup.

Intersex people are not a recent phenomenon, and there is good research to suggest that Judaism addressed this even before the time of Christ. When Jesus addressed people who were "born eunuchs" (Matthew 19 v 12), it is likely he was including or referring to intersex people. Yet, in this same passage, Jesus affirmed that gender is binary: "Have you not read that he who created them from the beginning made them male and female...?" (Matthew 19 v 4). Regardless of whether or not he included people who are intersex in the eunuch category, Jesus (who is God) affirmed that gender as God has created it is binary—a person is one or the other—so we must as well.

We shouldn't reason from the uncertain to the certain. We reason from the certain (God created them male and female) and then address the uncertain. Fundamentally, it comes down to this: has God spoken; was he right;

and is it authoritative? The only correct and consistent answer to those questions is "yes."

We have not fully addressed the existence of intersex people, but they are not in the same category as people with gender dysphoria.[1] *More importantly, the existence of a class of people doesn't tell us anything about the moral rightness of the actions of another group of people.* Just because some people have ambiguous genitals, it doesn't mean that it is a good thing for everyone else to choose their gender or be encouraged to act out of concert with their biology. That simply doesn't follow.

It's Not Intolerant to Disagree with Culture on Gender

While you likely already know this, if you take a clear and convictional stand on biblical gender, there's a good chance you will be called intolerant, hateful, transphobic, or bigoted. When someone calls you such a name, ask them, "What do you mean by that?" Often, people will end up giving a definition that applies equally well to themselves as it does to you. For instance, "What do you mean by intolerant?" "Well, you think you're right, and everyone else is wrong." You might then reply, "But don't you think you're right, and I'm wrong? Why is that not intolerant as well?"

Tolerance used to mean disagreeing with someone while still respecting them as a person, but we've lost this concept. The kind of "tolerance" our modern

---

1 See the definition for this term in the Glossary on page 73.

culture requires is that you say all views are equally valid; none is better than another. What seems lost on people who believe in the new tolerance is that if every view is equally valid, then so is your view that disagrees with theirs. The new tolerance is incapable of being consistently applied. Furthermore, tolerance implies disagreement. It doesn't make sense to say you tolerate something you agree with.

So, when someone claims that you're intolerant, ask them for a definition. Chances are good they aren't being tolerant (by their definition), either. True tolerance respects people in the midst of disagreement. Christians are called to speak God's truth into the dark voids of society and people's lives, and yet to do so with gentleness and respect. As we've already discussed, people are all created in the image of God, and we should treat them like that, even in the midst of disagreement.

Love Does Not Equal Affirmation

Many children (and adults) struggle to see the difference between love and affirmation. You can love someone without affirming what they are doing or what they believe. God loves us, but he doesn't affirm all of our actions. It is not uncommon to hear people claim that disagreeing about gender and sexuality is unloving. That is simply not the case. For more on this see "God wants me to be happy" in the "Objections" section below on page 65.

If you love someone, you will truly want what is best for them. Sometimes, people understand things they have heard and dislike to mean that the person who said them is hateful. But that is not always the case. Often, the people who love us most have the hardest things to say. Just because someone agrees with you on something does not mean that they love you. Just because someone disagrees with you does not mean that they do not love you.

Think of a doctor who discovers that a patient has an illness. The patient obviously wants to hear the doctor say, "All is well. We will see you again for another check-up next year!" The patient might even feel great, because they have no idea that the doctor knows there is something seriously wrong with them. I think we can agree that the doctor should not avoid telling the patient the truth, just to keep the patient feeling good. That would be malpractice. If the doctor cares, she will be honest and tell her patient the truth. When someone shares what they believe to be true, even if it disagrees with what you believe, that is not necessarily unloving.

The Ultimate Problem Is Not About Choosing a Different Gender Identity

Having a correct, biblically-informed understanding of gender is very important, but it is not the most important goal. If your child has a friend who is male, but identifies as female, that person's greatest need isn't to accept a male gender identity. Their greatest need is salvation: trusting in the good, creator God to forgive their sin by submitting to his lordship.

So, instead of simply trying to address the symptoms of a person's fallenness, we need to address the root cause, which is their lack of spiritual regeneration.

For example, if you have the opportunity to talk with someone close to you who struggles with their gender identity, you could say, "This may feel right, but God has created you male, not female, and while that's important, my heart for you is that you would come to know the God who created you."

All sin—not following God's word—is worthy of punishment by God. However, we don't want to suggest that the Christian message is that people need to just sin less in specific areas, and then they'll be seen favorably by God. That is not the gospel of grace; it is the false gospel of works. The only hope for every person—whether they've adopted a different gender identity, robbed a bank, or yelled at their parents—is to be clothed in the righteousness of Jesus, by trusting in him for the forgiveness of their sins.

JESUS AND THE GOSPEL

Regardless of what we believe about gender, we are all in need of Jesus. We have all been plagued with sin and need our failings to be covered up by the perfect righteousness of Christ. In order to see their need for Jesus, people first need to see their sin and brokenness. The gospel is level ground for us all. When we truly believe the gospel, we cannot look at others as if they are too broken or too far from God.

At the same time, we should care enough to humbly, lovingly, and carefully bring others to see their need for Jesus. Nothing could be more selfish or unloving than hiding the gospel from those around us.

An integral part of the gospel is trusting in Christ for salvation, but it is also crucial to trust the truthfulness of Christ's statements on the authority and reliability of scripture and God's male/female design of human beings.

When we are saved by God, we are not called out of the world. In John 17 Jesus prays that his followers would not be removed from the world, but rather, that they would be protected from Satan—the evil one—and his lies (v 15).

Jesus could have prayed for us to be as far away from the non-Christian world as possible, but he did not. He could have prayed that we completely ignore the world, but he did not. Jesus has not only saved us; he has called us to be a light of truth in this world. Part of being a follower of Jesus is being active in this world. When others disagree, we should not run away, but seek to point them to Christ. As challenging as that might be, it is what we are called to do.

AGE TIPS

- *Know where your student stands.* Parents need to be "students of their students." If you are going to help them build strong foundations in God's word and follow Christ in this world, you need to understand where they stand. It is important that you take the time to listen to them. Ask questions which will help you have an idea of what they believe and how they are thinking. Conversations are critical to helping bring clarity to students.

- *Understand what influences them.* One of the most challenging things about working with middle-school and high-school students is the sheer number of influences that surround their lives. They are being influenced by students in locker rooms, statements on social media, music on their phones, shows on Netflix, and what they are hearing at home. Most students want to get the big issues in life "right." They want to understand their purpose in the world and hold the correct views on sexuality and gender.

- *Students aren't necessarily looking to be led astray; they are just confused.* It is challenging because, although they want to "get it right," they are constantly being given multiple answers about what "right" is. We need to take the time to talk through the various voices they are hearing, and point them to the Bible with clarity and conviction. If we fail in clarity, we will lead them to confusion. If we fail in conviction, they will fail to care.

- *Always include the "why."* In middle school and high school, students begin to move from concrete thinking to abstract thinking. As they begin to think abstractly, they begin to focus more and more on the "why." (Why does God care what gender someone identifies with?) As we talk with students, we need to be sure to not just tell them what God's word says but *why* it all matters. If we fail to address the "why," they will either lose interest or ignore the Bible's teaching completely.

- *Friends may believe differently.* Parents need to resist the urge to train their children to shun those who believe differently than they do, while still guarding them from corrupting influences. The best way to do this is similar to how we approach vaccinations. Before traveling to India, you would likely get some shots, for without them you would may well get sick. But you get the shots, *and then you go to India.* Training our children in these areas can take a similar approach: inoculate your children by teaching them biblical truth and how other people disagree with it. Then, use life events as a springboard for further discussion.

- *You need to be more involved in shaping how your child thinks when they have friends who believe differently.* So, if your child has a friend who identifies as transgender, encourage your child to show the love of Christ to that person by not shunning them and by being kind. It's also a good opportunity to talk with your child about how we all have our sins and problems. We shouldn't avoid non-Christians because of their sin, but we should love them as people without taking a soft line on sin.

- *Stay proactive.* The cultural conversation about gender came about very suddenly, and it is changing quickly. There's always something in the news about it, and we're faced with the question: are we going to let culture frame the discussion, or are *we* going to frame the discussion?

- As previously mentioned, *talking about gender isn't a one-time conversation.* The constant bombardment of news stories and social events surrounding gender are good opportunities for discussion on the way home from school or as a family at dinner. As a family, try to find the faulty thinking, discuss what the Bible has to say, and decide what the kind and convictional Christian response should be.

QUESTIONS AND DISCUSSION STARTERS

- Why do you think our culture says you can be whatever gender you want?
- What do your friends believe about gender?
- Why do people reject the idea that there are only two genders? How would you respond?
- Do you know anyone who is transgender? What are they like? How do people respond to them?

What do you think is a good response to that person?

- How is it difficult believing differently than a lot of your classmates?
- What different identities do we have as people (e.g. ethnic, nationality, gender, work, interests)?
- How can we make sure that our identity in Christ is the most important?

USEFUL BIBLE PASSAGES TO READ AND DISCUSS

Parenting

- *Deuteronomy 11 v 19*. We need to teach our children what has been declared by the Lord.
- *Proverbs 22 v 6*. We need to raise our children in an intentional way that helps guide them through life.

Creation

- *Genesis 1 – 3*. God creates man and woman and calls them "very good." Having both genders was an intentional part of God's creation for His glory.
- *Matthew 19 v 4-6*. Jesus reinforces that God designed us "male and female."
- *Psalm 139 v 13*. tells us that God "knits us together" in the womb.
- *Romans 1 v 18-32*. Paul tells us that it is possible to choose "unnatural" desires that are not honoring to God. We are all in need of God's grace because we have all chosen to sin against him.

Worldview

- *Romans 12 v 2*. We need to be careful not to conform to the way the world thinks and sees.
- *Psalm 119 v 105*. God's word is meant to be a guide to our life. It may not answer every question specifically but it gives us the wisdom to know how to think about these things.

Trusting what Scripture Teaches

- *2 Timothy 3 v 16*. We can trust Scripture because it is from God and equips us to live for him and please him.
- *Jeremiah 17 v 9*. It is dangerous to "trust our hearts."
- *Ephesians 4 v 17-18*. Sin darkens our minds and distorts our understanding of how we should see the world and live.

Scripture That Needs Clarifying

- *Galatians 3 v 28*. God is not saying that gender no longer exists, since Paul also affirms different roles for each gender in Ephesians 5. He is saying, however, that all people are equal in their worth and standing before God, regardless of their gender.

A FINAL WORD FOR PASTORS AND PARENTS

Although we live in a broken world filled with confusion, we follow a risen Savior who has overcome this world and has given us his word. As Christian parents, and as those who have the responsibility for leading children and young people in church, God has called and equipped us for the task of training up our children to love and walk in the ways of our Lord. While your child might not struggle with their gender identity, they will almost certainly struggle with who they will listen to—Scripture or culture? By instilling in your child a firm foundation of biblical truth, they will be more likely to stand against the winds of cultural change that aim to bend them to conformity.

Be encouraged. You are not alone in your journey to raise godly children. Other parents and pastors in your local church are trying to do the same. Link arms with them and rely on each other. Ask for advice. Share your experiences and results as you try the suggestions in this guide.

Remember: it's never too late to start having these conversations, but it's never too early, either.

FOR ADULTS

UNDERSTANDING THE ISSUES
ANSWERING OBJECTIONS

Let's be honest: it can be awkward talking about gender and sexuality. It's awkward for the adult *and* for the child. But the discomfort shouldn't stop us from discussing these topics. If it does, we're effectively saying that our comfort is more important than instilling a biblical concept of gender and biblical authority in our children. If parents aren't the clearest voices to their children on these issues, culture will be.

When we see what is truly at stake—allegiance to God's word and his good design in creation—we can and must press through the awkwardness. Many of the important activities in life aren't easy or comfortable, but they can be rewarding and beneficial.

We can admit to our children that this may be awkward, but that it's important enough that we're going to talk about it. This models that discomfort shouldn't keep us from doing the right thing. Culture doesn't feel awkward talking to our children about gender, and neither should we.

RESTROOMS

Sometimes gender confusion is accompanied by a desire to use the restroom that matches a person's gender identity, not their biology. This has led to many controversies such as large retail chains adopting a policy where shoppers can use whichever bathroom they want. Likewise, many schools and colleges now allow students to use the bathroom that matches their chosen gender identity. So, the question becomes: how should Christians think about which bathrooms people use? It might seem odd that Christians should care at all, and genuine believers may have different views (see p 60), but there are several strong reasons to take a position on this.

First, there is a legitimate safety concern. When a bathroom is understood to have only female-looking people enter it, it is very easy to see when a male enters and shouldn't. With this removed, there is nothing stopping male predators from using the women's bathroom without arousing suspicion. This isn't to say by any means that trans people are predators; just that others who are will take advantage of bathroom access ceasing to be based on sex.

Second, as laws are made to allow people to use the bathroom of their chosen gender identity, it will necessarily infringe on the religious liberty of churches and business owners. Some cities/states have already tried to say that if churches are open to the public, they must let people use the restroom of their choice. This clearly infringes on the right of the church to structure its facilities in the way its convictions dictate.

Third, no one is being denied access to the bathroom; they just need to use the bathroom of their biological sex. This is why there are separate facilities for different sexes. The types of facilities match the types of anatomy. Bathrooms are designed to match bodies, not souls. Of course, there are privacy concerns, too, which is another reason for separate facilities. Biological girls shouldn't need to fear that their locker or changing room may be shared by biological men.

LANGUAGE MATTERS

Language really does matter. It allows us to communicate with each other about the world. Can you imagine trying to accomplish even simple tasks with other people without the use of any language? It would be impossible.

Because language is our way of describing the world, we will often disagree about word choice with people who see the world differently. For instance, when a person begins to identify as a different gender, they may wish to go by a different name—one that matches their new gender identity. Mark may wish to be called Mary. While it may feel odd, we should call people by the name they wish to be called, since names are arbitrary and made up.

Along with changing their name, a person who identifies as a different gender may wish for others to refer to them with the pronouns that match their new gender identity. So, instead of using "he" to refer to Mark, you could be asked to use "she" because you are now referring to Mary. Again, Christians will have different opinions on this (see page 60), but we think it is appropriate to call people by the *name* they choose, since we do not want to offend unnecessarily. But we believe it would be incorrect to refer to people with *pronouns* that do not match their biological sex. Because Mary is male (even though *he* identifies as female), we should still use male pronouns when referring to *him*.

Names are arbitrary and made up, but pronouns reflect the sex of a person *as they are created by God*. Pronouns are our way of describing the reality of a person's sex. Not all Christians agree that it's better to call people by the pronouns that match their sex rather than the ones that match their chosen gender identity. They would say that refusing to address someone as they request puts an unnecessary roadblock in the way of conversation. We appreciate this concern and respect their intent here.

However, it is important to realize that there are at least two audiences in conversations: there is, of course, the person we are speaking with (who may be unhappy about our choice of pronouns), but God is also an audience of how we speak about *his* world and his image bearers. For this reason, we should not intentionally speak about his creation differently than he does. When we refer to a biological male as a "woman" or as a "she," we fail to describe the world as it is and as God designed it to be.

That said, it is best to avoid using personal pronouns around a person if you disagree on which pronouns should be used. We should try to minimize offense when we can, while still being faithful to our convictions.

WHAT'S THE RISK?

While the obvious risk is that your child might find themselves confused, behind the curtain of this concern is the risk that your child will let culture lead them away from Scripture. With each day, culture becomes more opposed to a biblical view of sin, self, and sexuality. Inevitably, you and your children will have relationships with people who live in ways opposed to God's design. We *should* have relationships with people like this. If we don't build relationships with lost people, we drastically cut down on our chances of sharing the gospel with them.

The concern comes when someone your child is close to is transgender. Now, your child will likely feel the tension of being told that Christians are to love everyone, while at the same time holding the belief that this lifestyle choice is wrong. Frequently, this type of situation results in the Christian compromising their beliefs because of the relationship they have with the other person. This is why it is all the more important to start rooting your children in God's truth from a young age, and to model how to build relationships with those who disagree with your views.

So, the most pressing risk is not that your child becomes trans, but that this or another issue will drive a wedge between them and God's authoritative word. Christians don't have to buy the lie that you can either love your friends or agree with the Bible. We can and must do both.

WHAT DO WE DO WHEN CHRISTIANS DISAGREE?

Even though Christians have been regenerated by the Holy Spirit, we can still disagree on many things. There may be things you have read in this book that you disagree with. When it comes to addressing transgender questions, there are more and less important points of agreement. For instance, since Scripture is our authority, there is no room to contradict the truth that gender is binary. We must affirm that God made humans male and female. This is extremely clear.

On the other hand, views on how we engage the culture on this issue and what public policies we support or oppose may very well differ, even if we affirm God's design for mankind. One Christian may believe that trans people should use the bathroom of their choice; others may disagree. Someone may believe we should use the pronouns that a trans person prefers, and others may not.

There is certainly room for dialogue and discussion here. Maybe you'll change someone's mind, or maybe they'll change yours. But in all our discussions we must show grace and patience. But if someone disagrees on the nature of God's creative work in making humankind male and female, we must return to Scripture as our authority and encourage others to do the same.

HOW YOU SPEAK MATTERS

Along with the sexual revolution has come the tendency for people to base their identity and worth on their sexuality or gender identity. While we believe this is misguided, we must remember how deeply felt this is when talking with such people. When we disagree with their behavior or say it's wrong or against God's design, they often take this to mean that all of who they are is wrong or against God's design. While we still need to communicate biblical truth, we need to be conscious of how it is likely to be interpreted on these types of issues.

More than that, however, we cannot allow ourselves to see this only in terms of "issues" or "positions." These are real people—image-bearers of God—who are confused and hurting. When we discuss these topics, we have to remember that these struggles have names and faces. The trans person is not a potential argument to be won but a soul to be comforted and encouraged— a person who is lost in the darkness who we want to lead to the Light of the world. Ultimately, true rest is only found through the soul-transforming work of the Spirit, which accompanies belief in the gospel. We must be gracious and kind toward these people to show them the love of Jesus if we ever hope for them to listen to God's design and redemptive plan for them.

How we speak can either make or break our message, and our culture's sensitivity to our "tone" is higher than ever before. As pastor and author Tim Keller says:

> Love without truth is sentimentality; it supports and affirms us but keeps us in denial about our flaws. Truth without love is harshness; it gives us information but in such a way that we cannot really hear it. God's saving love in Christ, however, is marked by both radical truthfulness about who we are and yet also radical, unconditional commitment to us. The merciful commitment strengthens us to see the truth about ourselves and repent. The conviction and repentance moves us to cling to and rest in God's mercy and grace.
> The Meaning of Marriage (Penguin, 2013), page 40

May we be people who reflect our Lord's commitment to loving truthfully, and speaking truth lovingly.

ANSWERING OBJECTIONS

As you strive to teach and apply the concepts in this book, you will encounter objections. Some of these have been addressed along the way in their respective sections. We have included responses to some other, more general, objections below. While this is far from an exhaustive list, hopefully the way in which each objection is handled will serve as a model for responding to other potential objections. These objections may be repeated to you by a child who is a professing Christian and has struggled to answer a question posed to them by a friend at school or college. You can help nurture their faith and equip them to answer others and so fulfill the command:

> *Always be prepared to give an answer to everyone who asks you to give the reason for the hope that you have. But do this with gentleness and respect…*
>
> 1 Peter 3 v 15 (NIV)

"The Bible Is outdated"

Throughout this guide, we've been consistent in grounding our perspective in what the Bible says about God, creation, and gender. But for many people, this raises the question: why should I care about what a two-thousand-year-old book says about gender or life?

If it were simply a book like any other, you probably shouldn't care very much, but as 2 Timothy 3 v 16 says, all Scripture is the word of God, and as such there can be no higher authority. However, most people will not find it sufficiently compelling that Scripture claims to be the word of God. There are many additional reasons to believe that it is, though.

First, the manuscript evidence we have for the New Testament is early; we have copies from within 20 to 50 years of the time the original documents were written. We have thousands of copies from throughout the centuries, so we're able to see that the teaching of the Bible hasn't changed. How does this compare to other ancient works, you may ask? There are thousands more copies that are hundreds of years earlier than those for any other ancient work.

Second, the Bible contains eyewitness testimony, such as that of Peter and John. Luke talked with eyewitnesses to compile the books of Luke and Acts. How do we know they were actually there for the events they describe? They correctly cite locations, dialects, governors, customs, and more details that they would only know if they were where and when they claimed to be.

Third, the Bible contains details that would only have been included if they were true—you don't intentionally make up embarrassing stories. The biblical authors record that they doubted Jesus, denied him, fell asleep when he told them to pray, and failed to understand him. They wrote that Jesus' family thought he was crazy, and others thought he was a drunkard or even the devil. These are just a few of the embarrassing details in the Bible. No one makes up stories that make themselves look bad.

Fourth, the biblical authors were willing to endure torture and die for their claims. Unlike today's religious extremists, the biblical authors were actually in the position to know if their claims about Jesus were accurate; they witnessed what they claimed. Today's extremists don't have first-hand knowledge of their claims. Many people will die for something they believe to be true, but no one dies for something they *know* to be a lie.

For these and other reasons, Christians can trust that the Bible is God's word. Since God is perfect, his word is perfect too; it does not contain errors. The Bible doesn't leave open the possibility that Jesus was right about loving our neighbor, but wrong about how God created us to live and function.

The truth of how God created humans male and female doesn't change with time, and it doesn't become outdated. It was true two thousand years ago, and it is still trustworthy and true today.

"God wants me to be happy"

It's common to hear people say that God just wants them to be happy. Sadly, this message has seeped into the preaching and teaching of some churches too. The trouble is that the word "happy" is usually not defined. It's left up to each of us to define what happiness means for us. For one person "happy" might be having a big house and fancy car, and for someone else it might be a home full of family gathered around the dinner table. So, does God want us to be happy? To answer that, we must first answer two more general questions: does God want certain things for us, and how can we know if he does?

In order for us to know what God wants, he would have to reveal his desires to us. Thankfully, there is one such place where God has personally communicated about himself to us: the Bible.

> *All Scripture is breathed out by God and profitable for teaching, for reproof, for correction, and for training in righteousness, that the man of God may be complete, equipped for every good work.* 2 Timothy 3 v 16-17

In other words, Scripture gives us everything we need for doing good and being righteous. Yet, when we consult Scripture, we will never find God saying he wants us to be happy or even that one's personal happiness is the greatest good.

In Scripture, Jesus tells those who want to seek righteousness to deny themselves, pick up their cross, and follow him. Scripture also states that we were created to "image" (reflect) God's glory, and that our desires are often sinful—sin makes us happy. While we could certainly continue this list of Scriptural truths, one thing is clear: we were created to live for the glory of God, not for our own happiness. We are to be holy as he is holy.

When we die to ourselves daily and pursue godliness, we will actually find lasting, true joy. This is much more in line with what God has revealed in Scripture, since Jesus came so that we may have life, and have it abundantly. God created us to worship him, and he created us such that it is only when we glorify him that our souls are deeply satisfied. If we seek happiness, it will be fleeting, but if we seek holiness, we will find lasting joy.

Perhaps the easiest way to deal with this objection is to ask the objector: "How did you come to the conclusion that God just wants you to be happy?" Make them provide you with the reasons why you (and they) should hold that view. Most likely, they will say something about God being love, and that love means making someone happy. You can provide counter examples from scripture and daily life showing that love sometimes requires unpleasant actions, that are nonetheless loving.

"God made me this way"

While not always the case, often times the person who claims that their behavior is fine because "God made them that way" doesn't actually believe God created life; they believe in evolution. This is a major inconsistency: you can't claim God made you the way you are and deny his creative work in making you.

But even if that isn't the case, this claim proves too much. If God's creation of a person means that their desires and actions are acceptable, then how can we condemn murder, adultery, and rape? People who commit those actions have natural desires leading them to those actions. People who lie and gossip were made by God too, but this doesn't mean those actions are acceptable. You can never determine if something *should* be the case just by noticing that it *is* the case. Just because people lie, that doesn't mean lying is okay. And just because people have gender dysphoria, that doesn't mean changing one's gender is good either.

This and all claims should be subjected to the revealing light of Scripture. When God said he made humans "male and female" he was speaking, at the least, about their physical biology. There was no social construct of what boys or girls were supposed to be like at that point. What God said was male, was male because of biology. Nothing in Scripture ever points to this changing.

However, shortly after we see God create man and woman, they fall into sin and break the world. Their sin broke their relationship with God, their relationship with each other, and their own self-image. Everyone's nature is corrupted by sin, not just the trans person. We all have desires that are contrary to God's good design. So, yes, God made everything, and it was good. But that good creation (mankind) disobeyed God, and now everything in creation is spoiled or broken; things are not as they should be. And this is why we can't point to something in the world and say, "It *should* be this way because it *is* this way."

"Christians are closed-minded"

When someone calls you closed- or narrow-minded, before you start to defend yourself or disagree, ask them what they mean by "closed-minded." More than likely, they'll say something such as "You think you're right and everyone else is wrong." You could ask a second question then: "Do you think that you're right and I'm wrong?" since they clearly think you're wrong. Based on their definition, they're closed-minded too.

You could also ask why being closed-minded is wrong. If there are right and wrong answers to important questions, shouldn't we be very cautious in what views we adopt? The nature of truth is that it is narrow and exclusive. For so many questions in life, there is only one right answer, and there are a multitude of wrong answers. Should I take insulin or ice cream for my diabetes? Is the White House in Washington or Salt Lake City? Did Jesus rise from the dead or not? Did God create men and women distinctly different, yet complementary? There must be right and wrong answers to these questions. When people disagree on the answers, they are being equally narrow in their views.

Christians should not have closed minds on many issues, though. That is, we should evaluate the evidence and come to the best conclusions that we can. On every matter it speaks to, the Bible is the best evidence. As God's revelation to us, it is the highest authority. So, our views will necessarily be narrow. We should not have closed minds, but minds open to being filled with the word of God.

"If God forgives me and loves me, what's the big deal?"

"Jesus paid for our sin on the cross, right? So it doesn't matter how I live." When we're confronted with this claim, we should ask the person how they came to this conclusion. Have them make their case. The only way we could know such a thing is if God revealed it in Scripture. Thankfully, God addresses this claim in the New Testament.

In Romans 5, Paul tells us that all those who are in Christ have been declared righteous—right before God. Then, beginning in chapter 6, he answers what would be a natural question: if we've been declared righteous, "are we to continue in sin so that grace may abound?" To which Paul replies, "By no means!" We are to crucify the works of the flesh and anything that is opposed to the will of God.

Scripture also addresses the person who has been told the truth and unrepentantly keeps on sinning:

> *For if we go on sinning deliberately after receiving the knowledge of the truth, there no longer remains a sacrifice for sins, but a fearful expectation of judgment, and a fury of fire that will consume the adversaries.*
>
> Hebrews 10 v 26-27

If we do not desire to stop sinning, we should question whether or not we have the Holy Spirit, who works to reform our desires and makes us more like Christ.

"What if you are both genders?"

For the person asking this question, ask how they determined they were both genders. Most likely this will stem from how they feel. People are individuals, and we must talk with them as individuals with their individual concerns. For the non-Christian, the bigger concern is that they don't know Christ. For the Christian who is struggling with the belief that they are both genders, we should go to Scripture and see that God has created us *either* male or female.

When we have feelings that are out of concert with how God designed us, it is our job to work to align how we think and feel with how we are made to function. Paul speaks to this

> *We destroy arguments and every lofty opinion raised against the knowledge of God, and take every thought captive to obey Christ.* 2 Corinthians 10 v 5

We all have thoughts, feelings, and impulses that are dishonorable and against God's design. But our feelings don't always correctly inform us about reality.

I may feel that I am both genders, but that doesn't mean I am. Some people who are of a healthy weight feel that they are overweight even though they aren't; feeling that you're fat doesn't *make* you fat anymore than feeling that you're both genders makes you be both genders.

We shouldn't disregard the fact that feelings are real and powerful, even if they don't always inform us correctly.

Let's not dismiss the person who is gender-confused because "that's just a feeling they have." We need to walk with people and help them ground their identity in their createdness as an image-bearer of God and an adopted *son or daughter* in God's family.

FINAL WORDS OF ENCOURAGEMENT

These conversations aren't a "one-time thing." They're a "lifetime thing." This isn't to say that there aren't important and strategic times to sit down and have a discussion, but it must be understood that we have to be continually in conversation about gender in age-appropriate ways. Television and radio will not have a one-time talk with your child about gender. Social media will not have a one-time conversation with your child about gender. And you can be certain that the students in the hallway or in gym class won't have a one-time conversation about gender with your child. As Christians who believe what God's word says about gender, let's not be the ones who talk about it the least or last. Make it a point to have ongoing and appropriate conversations in your home.

Rather be too early than too late. We obviously want to be age-appropriate with children, but we also need to be proactive, not reactive. The nature of this guide is to help you start the conversation with your children before others do.

GLOSSARY

These definitions come from a pro-transgender site (stonewall.org.uk). While we have included the definitions as they were written, we reject the idea that sex is "assigned" at birth. A person's sex is intrinsic to their biology. We do not assign it; we describe it.

Cisgender or *Cis*. Someone whose gender identity is the same as the sex they were assigned at birth. Non-trans is also used by some people.

Gender dysphoria. Used to describe when a person experiences discomfort or distress because there is a mismatch between their sex assigned at birth and their gender identity. This is also the clinical diagnosis for someone who doesn't feel comfortable with the gender they were assigned at birth.

Gender identity. A person's internal sense of their own gender, whether male, female or something else (see non-binary below).

Gender reassignment. Another way of describing a person's transition. To undergo gender reassignment usually means to undergo some sort of medical intervention, but it can also mean changing names, pronouns, dressing differently, and living in their self-identified gender.

Intersex. A term used to describe a person who may have the biological attributes of both sexes or whose biological attributes do not fit with societal assumptions about what constitutes male or female. Intersex people can identify as male, female, or non-binary.

Non-binary. An umbrella term for a person who does not identify as male or female.

Pronoun. Words we use to refer to people's gender in conversation; for example, "he" or "she". Some people may prefer others to refer to them in gender-neutral language and use pronouns such as they / their and ze / zir.

Sex. Assigned to a person on the basis of primary sex characteristics (genitalia) and reproductive functions. Sometimes the terms "sex" and "gender" are interchanged to mean "male" or "female."

Trans, Tranny. An umbrella term to describe people whose gender is not the same as, or does not sit comfortably with, the sex they were assigned at birth. Trans people may describe themselves using one or more of a wide variety of terms, including (but not limited to) transgender, cross-dresser, non-binary, genderqueer (GQ).

Transgender man. A term used to describe someone who is assigned female at birth but identifies and lives as a man. This may be shortened to trans man, or FTM, an abbreviation for female-to-male.

Transgender woman. A term used to describe someone who is assigned male at birth but identifies and lives as a woman. This may be shortened to trans woman, or MTF, an abbreviation for male-to-female.

Transitioning. The steps a trans person may take to live in the gender with which they identify. Each person's transition will involve different things. For some this involves medical intervention, such as hormone therapy and surgeries, but not all trans people want or are able to have this. Transitioning also might involve things such as telling friends and family, dressing differently, and changing official documents.

Transphobia. The fear or dislike of someone who identifies as trans.

Transsexual. This was used in the past as a more medical term (similarly to homosexual) to refer to someone who transitioned to live in the "opposite" gender to the one assigned at birth. This term is still used by some, although many people prefer the term trans or transgender.

Source: www.stonewall.org.uk/help-advice/glossary-terms

OTHER RESOURCES

Further help on this subject can be found in these three helpful books:

Transgender by Vaughan Roberts
(The Good Book Company, 2016)

God and the Transgender Debate by Andrew T. Walker
(The Good Book Company, 2017)

Is God Anti Gay? by Sam Allberry
(The Good Book Company, 2013)

A TALKING POINTS BOOK BY
VAUGHAN ROBERTS

TRANSGENDER

There's been huge cultural change in the last few decades. Same-sex marriage would have been unthinkable 20 or 30 years ago. Suddenly the issue of transgender is the next big social, cultural issue that is dominating the headlines.

Vaughan Roberts surveys the Christian world-view and seeks to apply its principles to the many complex questions surrounding gender identity. This short book gives an overview and a starting point for constructive discussion as we seek to live in a world with different values.

"In this brief book on a complex subject, Vaughan Roberts combines the traditional Christian understanding of gender and the body with a very careful, loving, understanding stance toward transgender people. The two almost never go together, and that's why this book is so good!"

Tim Keller, pastor, author, and Vice-President of
The Gospel Coalition

ANDREW T. WALKER

GOD AND THE
TRANSGENDER DEBATE

What is transgender and gender fluidity? What
does God's word actually say about these
issues? How can the gospel be good news for
someone experiencing gender dysphoria? How
should churches respond?

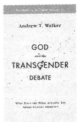

This warm, faithful, and careful book helps
Christians understand what the Bible says
about gender identity. It will help us to engage
lovingly, thoughtfully, and faithfully with one of the most
explosive cultural discussions of our day.

> *"This book resonates with gospel clarity and gospel compassion.*
> *It will empower you to share the good news of Jesus with those*
> *who grapple with gender-identity issues. The book is smart,*
> *wise, persuasive, and practical."*

Russell Moore, President, The Southern Baptist Ethics and
Religious Liberty Commission

thegoodbook.com | thegoodbook.uk
thegoodbook.com.au | thegoodbook.co.nz

thegoodbook
COMPANY

BIBLICAL | RELEVANT | ACCESSIBLE

At The Good Book Company, we are dedicated to helping Christians and local churches grow. We believe that God's growth process always starts with hearing clearly what he has said to us through his timeless word—the Bible.

Ever since we opened our doors in 1991, we have been striving to produce resources that honor God in the way the Bible is used. We have grown to become an international provider of user-friendly resources to the Christian community, with believers of all backgrounds and denominations using our Bible studies, books, evangelistic resources, DVD-based courses, and training events.

We want to equip ordinary Christians to live for Christ day by day, and churches to grow in their knowledge of God, their love for one another, and the effectiveness of their outreach.

Call us for a discussion of your needs or visit one of our local websites for more information on the resources and services we provide.

Your friends at The Good Book Company

NORTH AMERICA
UK & EUROPE
AUSTRALIA
NEW ZEALAND

 thegoodbook.com
thegoodbook.co.uk
thegoodbook.com.au
thegoodbook.co.nz

866 244 2165
0333 123 0880
(02) 9564 3555
(+64) 3 343 2463

 WWW.CHRISTIANITYEXPLORED.ORG
Our partner site is a great place for those exploring the Christian faith, with a clear explanation of the good news, powerful testimonies and answers to difficult questions.